BAINTE DEN STOC

WITHDRAWN FROM DLR LIBRARIES STOCK

NASCAR BLAST

DAVID CLAYTON

Crabtree Publishing Company

www.crabtreebooks.com

Crabtree Publishing Company
PMB 16A,
350 Fifth Avenue,
Suite 3308
New York, NY 10118

616 Welland Avenue,
St. Catharines, Ontario
L2M 5V6

Content development by
Shakespeare Squared

www.ShakespeareSquared.com

Published by Crabtree
Publishing Company © 2008

First published in Great Britain
in 2008 by ticktock Media Ltd,
2 Orchard Business Centre,
North Farm Road,
Tunbridge Wells, Kent, TN2 3XF

ticktock project editor:
  Ruth Owen
ticktock project designer:
  Sara Greasley
ticktock picture researcher:
  Lizzie Knowles

No part of this publication may be reproduced, copied, stored
in a retrieval system or transmitted in any form or by any means
electronic, mechanical, photocopying, recording or otherwise
without prior written permission of the copyright owner.

Copyright © ticktock Entertainment Ltd 2008

With thanks to: Series Editors Honor Head and Jean Coppendale

Picture credits (t=top; b=bottom; c=centre; l=left; r=right):
Action Plus: 8. Bettman/ Corbis: 22b. Jon Feingersh/
Getty Images: 14-15. Jonathan Ferrey/ Getty Images
for NASCAR: 13t. Focus on Sport/ Getty Images: 4t.
Richard Francis/ Action Plus: 7. Getty Images: 24, 31.
Chris Graythen/ Getty Images: 4-5 main. Jeff Hayes/
AFP/ Getty Images: 26-27. Chris McGrath/ Getty Images:
12, 13b. Chris O'Meara/ AP/ PA Photos: 23t. James
Powell: 18-19 main. RacingOne/ Getty Images: 6b.
Reuters/ Corbis: 23b, 29. Reuters/ Pierre Ducharme: 19t.
Reuters/ Charles W Luzier: 10-11. Sam Sharpe/ The
Sharpe Image/ Corbis: 16-17. Shutterstock: 1, 2. Jason
Smith/ Getty Images for NASCAR: 20-21.
ticktock Media Archive: 6t. George Tiedemann/ GT
Images/ Corbis: OFC, 5t, 9t, 22t, 25, 28l.

Every effort has been made to trace copyright holders, and we
apologize in advance for any omissions. We would be pleased to
insert the appropriate acknowledgments in any subsequent edition
of this publication.

Library and Archives Canada Cataloguing in Publication

Clayton, David, 1940-
    NASCAR blast / David Clayton.

(Crabtree contact)
Includes index.
ISBN 978-0-7787-3810-7 (bound).--ISBN 978-0-7787-3832-9 (pbk.)

    1. NASCAR (Association)--Juvenile literature. 2. Stock car
racing--United States--Juvenile literature. 3. Stock car drivers--
United States--Biography--Juvenile
literature. I. Title. II. Series.

GV1029.9.S74C54 2008   j796.72   C2008-901216-X

Library of Congress Cataloging-in-Publication Data
Clayton, David.
    NASCAR blast / David Clayton.
        p. cm. -- (Crabtree contact)
    Includes index.
    ISBN-13: 978-0-7787-3832-9 (pbk. : alk. paper)
    ISBN-10: 0-7787-3832-9 (pbk. : alk. paper)
    ISBN-13: 978-0-7787-3810-7 (reinforced library binding : alk. paper)
    ISBN-10: 0-7787-3810-8 (reinforced library binding : alk. paper)
    1. Stock car racing--United States--Juvenile literature. 2. Stock car
drivers--United States--Biography--Juvenile literature. 3. NASCAR
(Association)--Juvenile literature. I. Title.

    GV1029.9.S74C57 2008
    796.72--dc22

                                                    200800629

Contents

CHAPTER 1

THIS IS NASCAR

SPEED!

1987 – Bill Elliott does over three miles (4.8 km) a minute in his Thunderbird. He has a fastest lap of 212 miles per hour (341 kilometers per hour).

SPILLS!

2005 – Every race has its crashes. A 25-car pile-up at the Talladega **circuit** in 2005 was one of the worst. Thankfully, no one was hurt!

STARS!

2005 — Jeff Gordon wins at Daytona again. Gordon's race tactics mean NASCAR fans either love him or hate him!

NASCAR stands for **N**ational **A**ssociation of **S**tock **C**ar **A**uto **R**acing.

CHAPTER 2

CIRCUITS AND RACES

THEN...

The first NASCAR races started in 1948 at Daytona, Florida. Daytona was a 1.6 mile (2.6 km) beach-and-road circuit.

Souped-up passenger cars, such as Oldsmobiles, were soon the standard NASCAR racer.

1950 — NASCAR driver Red Byron races on Daytona Beach in a souped-up Oldsmobile

NOW...

Daytona is the top **venue** of the NASCAR race season. It is the first venue of the 37 races that make up the season.

Race crew's trailers, equipment, and camper vans

Track length is 2.5 miles (4 km)

Tailgating area for fans

Grandstand — the start and finish of the race

NASCAR holds three competitions:

- The Sprint Cup Championship (the top drivers)
- The Nationwide Series (2nd-level drivers)
- The Craftsman Truck Challenge

There are four different types of track — Short Speedway, Speedway, Superspeedway, and road circuits.

*North Carolina Speedway — a crash happens on the **banked** track.*

Speedways are all banked, left-hand-turn race tracks. They have concrete or **tarmac** surfaces.

Road circuits are normal roads that have been closed for a race. They are a tough test of a driver's skills. On road circuits, drivers have to make left-hand and right-hand turns.

Martinsville is a Short Speedway circuit. It is the shortest of all the circuits at 0.5 miles (1.6 km) long.

Martinsville Speedway, Virginia

Talladega Superspeedway, in Alabama, is the longest and fastest circuit. It is 2.6 miles (4.2 km) long.

NASCAR TRACKS

Short Speedways:	under 1 mile (less than 1.6 km)
Speedways:	1 to 2 miles (1.6-3.2 km)
Superspeedways:	over 2 miles (more than 3.2 km)
Road circuits:	over 1 mile (more than 1.6 km)

Kevin Harvick wins the 49th Daytona 500 NEXTEL Cup Series in 2007

SPRINT CUP RACE

There are always 43 drivers in a race. The winning driver of a race scores **185 points**. All of the other drivers score points, too, down to the driver in 43rd place, who gets 37 points.

Five bonus points are given to any driver who leads a lap. The driver who leads the most laps gets another five bonus points.

When 10 events remain in the Championship, the scoring gets a **SHAKE UP!** The 12 drivers with the most points are given a new, fresh score of 5,000 points. They are also given 10 points for each of their wins so far in the season.

Now, the top-12 drivers begin a new fight for the top spot! This keeps the **competition hot** between the top-12 drivers to the end of the season.

The drivers in 13th place and below are now too far behind the top 12 in points. They cannot win the championship. But they can still win single races.

CHAPTER 3

THE RACE
THE PIT CREW

Pit crews work long hours. They work away from home — always on the move.

Early on race day, every crew member checks out the pit and equipment. They check hoses, tools, computers, **compressed air**, windshield brushes, **video links**, lug nuts, and spare tires.

The pit is ready by 8 am.
There are only fuel cans left to fill.

The car is ready to race!

NASCAR rules say what size the car can be, how low to the ground it can be, and what type of fuel can be used. After the race, officials check to make sure no rules have been broken.

Then the cars are loaded onto trucks and...

...it's on the road again.

IN THE HOT SEAT!

The crowds have been at the venue since dawn. The pit crew has done its final checks.

It's time to go!

*It's 120° Fahrenheit (49° Celsius) in the cockpit and you are wearing a **Nomex** fire suit.*

The **pace car** leads you around the track.
The **green flag** comes down. In seconds you're doing
180 miles per hour (290 km/h).
You're **pulling 3G** on the curves, so you feel like you weigh
600 pounds (272 kilograms).
The **pit chief** and **spotter** shout instructions in your earphones.

CRASH!

The cars are three wide and...

...you're flying!

"We win some, lose some, and wreck some."
Dale Earnhardt

But one mistake and...

...you really ARE flying!

TACTICS

To save gas, you've got to "draft". This is when you get in close to the other cars to break the force of air.

It gives you a "**slingshot**" effect when you want to pull out and pass the other cars.

Getting close to the other cars has its dangers. You can get a nudge! Then you will be **aero loose** or **aero tight**.

The blue arrows show the flow of air

Car 56 gets a free ride from car 79 thanks to drafting

Aero loose is when the back end of the car breaks away. **Aero tight** is when the car won't turn. Worn tires can cause these to happen, too.

Aero loose

There's no time to react because you are going so fast.

You're just GONE!

PITTING

If a **yellow** **caution flag** is waved during the race, you get the chance to gas up or change tires.

You should do this early in the race. Then you will have plenty of gas and good tires to see you through the rest of the race. You want to avoid coming off the track later on in the race.

Front tire changer

Jack man

Front tire carrier

Every second that you're off the track costs you positions and points.

If the car needs repairs, your pit chief will call you in. The pit crew works as a team to do the job fast. Only seven crew members are allowed **"over the wall"** when you pit.

A perfect pit stop should last less than 10 seconds!

Gas catch man

Gas man

Rear tire carrier

Rear tire changer

CHAPTER 4

DRIVERS

RICHARD PETTY

- Over 1,000 races
- 200 wins
- 7 championships
- Retired 1992

"No one wants to quit when he's losing and no one wants to quit when he's winning."
Richard Petty

"Petty broke too many bones to count. He drove with cracked ribs, and even a broken neck. He was racing cool — the fans' favorite."
Tom Jensen — sports writer

DALE EARNHARDT
"THE INTIMIDATOR"

- 676 races
- 76 wins
- 7 championships
- Died, aged 49, in the 2001 Daytona 500.

"You've got to be closer to the edge than ever to win. That means sometimes you go over the edge."
Dale Earnhardt

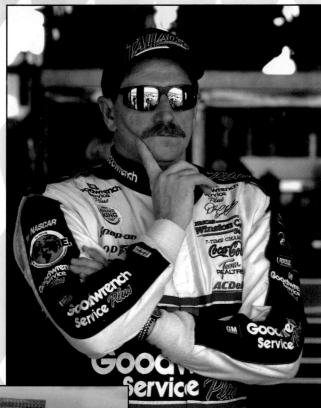

Dale Earnhardt Junior won at Daytona just five months after his father died there.

JEFF GORDON — LOVE HIM OR HATE HIM?

• 541 races
• 81 wins
• 4-time champion
(at the end of 2007 season)

Jeff Gordon won his first big race when he was only 22.

Fans either love Jeff Gordon or hate him.

One fan says:

> "Jeff drives clean against those who have earned it. He plays rough with those who have asked for it!"

Jeff Gordon (car 24) and Matt Kenseth — 2007 NEXTEL Cup

For example, in 2006, Jeff Gordon clashed with Matt Kenseth at Bristol, Tennessee. Jeff spun out!

At Chicago, Kenseth led until late in the race. Then he spun off after a nudge by...

...you guessed it. Jeff Gordon!

NASCAR has made the "Car of Tomorrow" its official design for 2008.

All Sprint Cup cars will be made to this design for future races.

New features:

- The body is wider and taller.

- Driver's seat and **roll cage** are more central for extra safety.

- **Crumple zone** is larger for extra safety.

- The exhaust system is further from driver.

- Rear wing is larger.

- Bumpers are standard height so they won't flip other cars.

- Less **aerodynamic** so

Colombian driver Juan Pablo Montoya with the new Dodge Avenger

CHAPTER 6

THE NATIONWIDE SERIES AND TRUCK RACING

The Nationwide Series car races and Craftsman truck races run on Fridays and Saturdays.

Nationwide Series cars

On Sundays, the big Sprint Cup race takes place on the same track.

The truck races are for **modified** pick-up trucks. The races are run over 150 to 250 miles (241.4 km– 402.3 km). These races began at Daytona in 1994.

The truck drivers play rough, too!

NASCAR — the loudest, roughest, toughest motor sport in the world!

NEED-TO-KNOW WORDS

aerodynamic A shape that helps a car cut through the air. This produces less drag so the car goes faster.

banked A track that is sloped

caution or yellow flag Flag shown after a crash or if there is garbage on the track. No passing is allowed at this time.

circuit A track for racing

compressed air Air under pressure produced by a machine. It is used to unscrew wheel nuts.

crumple zone Car body that bends to take the shock of a crash

gas catch man The man who stops gas from spilling in the pit

green flag The signal for the race to start

modified A car that has been changed and made more powerful

Nomex Fireproof material used to make race suits

"over the wall" Standing in the pit lane with the racing car

pace car A fast, powerful car that leads a parade of race cars when they need to remain below racing speed

pulling Gs The outward pull on your body when you go around corners

pit chief The team boss

roll cage Metal bars inside the car to stop the driver being crushed in a crash

souped-up A car in which the standard engine has been made faster

sponsor Companies who pay for the car and back-up services

spotter A man high above the track who warns his driver of trouble ahead

slingshot Something that gives a catapult effect

tailgating Partying and camping in the back of a car or truck during a NASCAR weekend

tarmac A hard road surface made from crushed rocks and tar

3G A pull three times the force of gravity

venue The place where an event is held

video links: Live TV pictures of the race. The pit crews watch the video links to check for trouble, such as worn tires or damage to the car.

How do I become a NASCAR Sprint Cup race car driver?

- Most drivers start young. Some start as early as 4 years old. They begin by racing karts or midget racing cars at their local racetracks.

2005 – World Midget Series, New Zealand

- Talent will soon have you moving up from amateur local races to events **sponsored** by big-name companies.

- Keep trying, and you may catch the eye of a big-name team like Hendrick Motorsports. They are always looking for new talent. In 2007, Hendrick had the top-two drivers in NASCAR.

- You need a desire to succeed and the energy and ambition to work hard. Being a good mechanic will help, too!

- Speaking well on TV will get you sponsors. Jeff Gordon (Hendrick) has sponsors such as Du Pont, Haas Automation, Bosch, and Pepsi! You can see their logos on his car and clothes.

And finally, you must keep fit!

NASCAR online

http://www.nascar.com/
The latest news about the drivers and the races

http://nascar.factexpert.com/1325-nascar-websites.php
Everything you want to know about NASCAR racing with useful links

www.nascarfans.wetpaint.com/page/NASCAR+Drivers+Websites
All the latest driver information for NASCAR fans

Publisher's note to educators and parents:
Our editors have carefully reviewed these websites to ensure that they are suitable for children. Many websites change frequently, however, and we cannot guarantee that a site's future contents will continue to meet our high standards of quality and educational value. Be advised that children should be closely supervised whenever they access the Internet.

Index

A
aero loose 18-19
aero tight 18-19

B
Bill Elliott 4

C
caution flag 20
cockpit 14
Craftsman Truck Challenge 8
crash 4, 8, 16, 30

D
Dale Earnhardt (The Intimidator) 23
Dale Earnhardt Junior 17, 23
Daytona International Speedway 5, 6-7, 10, 23, 29
Dodge Avenger 27
draft 18

E
equipment 7, 12

G
gas catch man 21
grandstand 7

J
jack man 20
Jeff Gordon 5, 24-25

L
left-hand turn 8

K
Kevin Harvick 10

M
Martinsville Speedway 9

N
Nationwide Series 8, 28
North Carolina Speedway 8

O
officials 13
Oldsmobile 6

P
pace car 15
pile-up 4
pit crew 12, 14, 20-21
pit stop 21

R
race crew 7
Red Byron 6
Richard Petty 22
right-hand turn 8
rules 13

S
scoring 11
slingshot 18
spotter 15
Sprint Cup 8, 10-11, 24, 26, 28, 31

T
tactics 18
Talladega Superspeedway 4, 9
Thunderbird 4
Tom Jensen 22
track 7, 8-9, 15, 20
truck 8, 28-29
tire changer 20-21

32